GALE
CENGAGE Learning

M000211905

Drama for Students, Volume 35

Project Editor: Kristen A. Dorsch Rights Acquisition and Management: Ashley Maynard, Carissa Poweleit Composition: Evi Abou-El-Seoud

Manufacturing: Rita Wimberley

Imaging: John Watkins

© 2018 Gale, A Cengage Company

For product information and technology assistance, contact us at **Gale Customer Support, 1-800-877-4253**.

For permission to use material from this text or product, submit all requests online at **www.cengage.com/permissions**.

Further permissions questions can be emailed to **permissionrequest@cengage.com** While every effort has been made to ensure the reliability of the information presented in this publication, Gale, A Cengage Company, does not guarantee the accuracy of the data contained herein. Gale accepts no payment for listing; and inclusion in the publication of any organization, agency, institution, publication, service, or individual does not imply endorsement of the editors or publisher. Errors brought to the attention of the publisher and verified to the satisfaction of the publisher will be corrected in future editions.

Gale
27500 Drake Rd.
Farmington Hills, MI, 48331-3535

ISBN-13: 978-1-4103-2833-5
ISSN 1094-9232

This title is also available as an e-book.
ISBN-13: 978-1-4103-9276-3
ISBN-10: 1-4103-9276-3
Contact your Gale, A Cengage Company sales

representative for ordering information.

Printed in Mexico
1 2 3 4 5 6 7 22 21 20 19 18

A View from the Bridge

Arthur Miller 1955

Introduction

A View from the Bridge, by famed American playwright Arthur Miller, is a psychological family tragedy set in the largely Italian neighborhood of Red Hook, Brooklyn. The play is retrospectively narrated by a lawyer, Alfieri, who makes clear from his opening monologue that the episode in question came to an unfortunate end. It revolves around a longshoreman—a laborer who loads and unloads docked ships— named Eddie, who must cope with two challenging transitions in his life: his beloved niece's reaching maturity and starting to make her own way in the world, and his wife's welcoming two Sicilian cousins to stay with them in a time of need. Despite having several interactions with Eddie, Alfieri can do little more than stand by as the dramatic tale unfolds.

As Miller related in other settings, the foundation for the play was a story told to him by a real-life lawyer in the Brooklyn waterfront area named Vinnie Longhi, about a man who found himself in precisely the situation described for Eddie. Initially shying away from the story, which he heard in 1947 and which seemed already too complete, Miller at last returned to it with the first one-act production of *A View from the Bridge*, which debuted at New York's Coronet Theater on September 29, 1955. Not entirely satisfied, Miller revised and extended the play, in part by changing monologues originally written in free verse or blank verse into prose, for a twoact production staged at London's Comedy Theatre beginning October 11, 1956. The original version is the one found in *A View from the Bridge: Two One-Act Plays* (1955). The two-act version, which is discussed here, is found in Miller's *Eight Plays* (1981) and other omnibus editions, such as *The Penguin Arthur Miller: Collected Plays* (2015).

Author Biography

Arthur Asher Miller Was Born On October 17, 1915, In Manhattan, New York City, To A Welloff Jewish Couple Who Lived In Then-Prosperous Harlem. His Father Owned A Coat-Manufacturing Business. The Young Arthur Was Not Inclined Toward Intellectual Pursuits, Preferring Almost Anything That Involved Physical Activity. He Enjoyed Playing Baseball And Football, Ice Skating, And Swimming, And By His Teen Years He Was Dabbling In Carpentry—Gaining Enough Skill To Build A Back Porch For His Family'S Home. The Family Moved To The Relatively Rural Midwood Area Of Brooklyn In 1929, As The Coat Business First Slackened, Then Collapsed Entirely With The Stock-Market Crash That Year. Common Labor Soon Became A Mainstay Of Miller'S Youngadult Life; Over The Next Few Years He Would Hold Jobs Ranging From Bakery Delivery Boy, Dishwasher, And Waiter To Warehouse Clerk, Truck Driver, And Factory Hand. After He Graduated From High School, He Took A Position As A Clerk, During Which Time He First Found Himself Engrossed In Literature—Starting, Of All Places, With *The Brothers Karamazov*, Fyodor Dostoevsky's greatest masterpiece. Miller suddenly felt that he was born to be a writer.

Successfully arguing that his poor high school grades did not reflect his capacities, Miller enrolled at the University of Michigan as a journalism student in 1934. He once joked that he chose journalism because he heard that that department gave out prizes—and indeed he proceeded to start winning prizes, not for journalism but for plays that he wrote. He won the university's Avery Hopwood Award for best play of the year twice, and another honor earned him a substantial cash prize and brought his work to the stage in Detroit. Graduating in 1938 and returning to New York, he worked with the Depression-era Federal Theatre Project and married his college sweetheart, Mary Grace Slattery, with whom he would have two children. He began writing and selling radio plays as well as film scripts—and thereby realizing how beholden scriptwriters were to the advertisers and executives of the stations and companies that produced them. During World War II, though he was unable to serve in the military due to an old injury, Miller toured army camps and wrote both a fictional movie and a nonfiction book based on the experience. His first Broadway play, *The Man Who Had All the Luck*, was produced in 1944; its run lasted less than a week.

Miller's level of success rose over the course of the following decade. He won the New York Drama Critics' Circle Award for *All My Sons* (1947) and that same award as well as the Pulitzer Prize for Drama for his renowned *Death of a Salesman* (1949). His works were steadily adapted for radio, television, and film, sometimes by himself, and his presence in Hollywood allowed him to meet the woman who, after he divorced his first wife, became his second, film star Marilyn Monroe. *A*

View from the Bridge (1955) represented the height of his success—not because his talents waned after that, but because he became a target of the House Un-American Activities Committee (HUAC) and Senator Joseph McCarthy's dogged hunt for Communist sympathizers. Miller had indeed supported far-left political causes, some of which involved the Communist Party, but only until 1950, and he declared before HUAC in 1956 that he would no longer support a Communist cause. What became a bigger problem was his morally upstanding refusal to name names of others who had participated in the same activities he had. He was ultimately convicted of contempt of Congress in 1957 and fined, though the following year an appeal reversed the conviction. Miller wrote very little during this period, and though his career was far from over, his greatest works were behind him.

In the last several decades of his life, Miller published additional plays as well as journals, short stories, and essays. His later plays were produced in such esteemed sites as the Lincoln Center Repertory Theater, but not on Broadway. In his personal life, he divorced Monroe and in 1962 married photographer Ingeborg Morath, with whom he would have two more children. He held a number of highly esteemed positions—including president of PEN and delegate to Democratic National Conventions— and eventually lived mainly in his country home in Roxbury, Connecticut. He died there of congestive heart failure at the age of eightynine on February 10, 2005.

Plot Summary

Act One

   A View from the Bridge opens on a set with multiple stage areas: in the center is the living/dining room area of Eddie and Beatrice's apartment, to the front and sides are the street outside the apartment building, to the right is a desk representing Mr. Alfieri's law office, and there is also a telephone booth. Mr. Alfieri enters, passes two men on the street, and stations himself inside his office at his desk. He speaks directly to the audience—he is both character and narrator—about the seedy nature of the Red Hook docks area of Brooklyn and his quirky interest in working there. He suggests that the fascinating case the audience will soon witness led to a bloody end.

   Having entered on the street, Eddie chats briefly with his friends Louis and Mike and then heads into the apartment. His niece, Catherine, is buoyant about a new skirt and plans to go out. Eddie judgmentally expresses his concerns about the attention she has been attracting from men on the street, almost bringing her to tears. Changing the subject, he announces that Beatrice's cousins have arrived, which sends Beatrice into a panic, because she has not fully prepared the apartment, having expected them the following week. Eddie expresses his concern that the cousins' staying with them will lead to his sleeping on the floor, so Beatrice coddles him.

Media Adaptations

- Renzo Rossellini composed an Italian opera based on Miller's play, *Uno sguardo dal ponte*, with the libretto adapted by Gerardo Guerrieri. The opera premiered on March 11, 1961, in Rome, and the first US performance came in Philadelphia on October 17, 1967.

- A 1962 film bearing the French title *Vu du pont* was directed by Sidney Lumet and produced by Transcontinental Films, with an adapted screenplay by Norman Rosten and a running time of 110 minutes. The film was released in the United States with Miller's original title.

- A New Zealand production of Miller's play directed by Ivo van Hove on July 5, 2015, was released as *National Theatre Live: A View from the Bridge*.

Catherine excitedly reports having gotten a stenographer's job at a local plumbing company, but Eddie objects—though he softens at mention of the pay of fifty dollars per week. Still, he had wanted her to get a classier job, to help her move up in the world. Eddie finally agrees to let her take the job, but he specifies that she should not trust any of the men there. Regarding the cousins, when Catherine asks Eddie what to do if someone asks about them, he insists that everyone must say absolutely nothing; apparently they are undocumented immigrants. When Catherine steps out to get Eddie a cigar, he and Beatrice show signs of relational stress, both imagining that the other has been angry.

When the lights go down on the scene, Alfieri appears now at the front of the stage, affirming that Eddie was a good man. The cousins had come at ten o'clock.

A friend named Tony escorts Marco and Rodolpho to the apartment door and leaves them there. They knock, Eddie lets them in, and they all make introductions. Marco thanks Beatrice and Eddie for letting him and his brother live with them for the time being. He wants to send as much money as possible home to his malnourished wife and three children in Sicily. Eddie starts to show a dislike of Rodolpho, who is boisterous with laughter and questions, while Catherine shows particular interest in him. Rodolpho dreams of being a motorcycle messenger working grand hotels in Italy. He is also a singer, and he demonstrates his talent with the jazz song "Paper Doll." Eddie politely suggests that being quieter would be prudent. When Eddie notices that Catherine is wearing high heels, he tells her to change; when she comes back, she offers Rodolpho sugar for his coffee.

The scene ends, and Alfieri ponders the fact that Eddie, though he could not have anticipated it, turned out to have a destiny. Weeks passed, and he was troubled.

As Beatrice approaches the house, Eddie, standing in the doorway, mentions that it is after eight, and she suggests that the movie at the Paramount ran long. In response to his questions, she reveals that Catherine is indeed thinking about marriage. In turn, Eddie questions Rodolpho's behaving like "a weird," occasionally bursting out in song and making everyone laugh too much. Beatrice expresses her own concern about when she is going to "be a wife again"— that is, when they will renew intimate physical relations. He evades the line of questioning and reaffirms his doubts about Rodolpho's character.

Beatrice goes inside, and Louis and Mike pass by. Mike's comments seem to confirm the strange impression Eddie has gotten of Rodolpho. As the two longshoremen leave, Catherine and Rodolpho return. Though Eddie expresses not wanting Catherine to go outside of Brooklyn, Rodolpho starts trying to persuade Eddie to let them go to Broadway. Soon Rodolpho goes for a walk, leaving Eddie to chat alone with Catherine. He eventually declares that Rodolpho is using her to get a passport, and she enters the house sobbing indignantly. Beatrice chews Eddie out, and he goes for a walk. Beatrice counsels Catherine to take her life into her own hands and marry Rodolpho.

The lighting shifts, and Eddie arrives at Alfieri's office. After Alfieri narrates his impressions upon Eddie's entrance, he turns and picks up the conversation at the point where Eddie has just finished explaining the situation with his niece. Alfieri does not understand whether Eddie has any question actually concerning the law. Eddie reiterates his uncomfortable feelings about Rodolpho, but Alfieri advises him to let the situation alone, because he has no legal recourse—presuming that he does not want to threaten their presence in America by calling immigration officials. Eddie acknowledges that he does not. Alfieri suggests that Eddie loves Catherine too much, that a man raising a niece to maturity might get mixed up about his feelings for her. Eddie sidesteps the implicit accusation by returning to the question of Rodolpho's character. Eddie departs, and Alfieri narrates how he was left feeling very alarmed, though there were yet no concrete misdeeds to point to.

Eddie, Beatrice, Catherine, Marco, and Rodolpho are finishing dinner. The Italians regale the Americans with stories of the old world. As they speak of how "free" things are with regard to men and women in America, Eddie indicates that Rodolpho has in fact been feeling too free with Catherine and gets riled up about the situation. When he calms down and sits on his rocker, Catherine provocatively puts "Paper Doll" on the phonograph and asks Rodolpho to dance. As Eddie gets tense again, it comes out that Rodolpho is also an excellent cook, and Eddie flares up once more. He suggests that what the men should really all do is go to a boxing match, and he prods Rodolpho into taking an impromptu lesson. They jab lightly at first, but Eddie escalates the intensity until getting a square blow to Rodolpho's face. Rodolpho shakes it off and resumes dancing with Catherine. Marco challenges Eddie to pick a chair up by the bottom of one leg, but Eddie cannot; Marco can, lifting the chair threateningly over Eddie's head and smiling. The curtain drops.

Act Two

Alfieri, at his desk, narrates that on December 23, a case of whisky slipped out of its net on the docks. Beatrice was shopping, Marco was working, and Rodolpho, who was not hired that day, was left home with Catherine.

Rodolpho mentions the money he has saved up, and Catherine asks whether he would want to take her back to Italy. He balks, wondering why he would leave a rich country to bring a wife to a poor country while having no job or prospects. When she asks whether he would still marry her if they had to go back, he replies that he would not marry her only to bring her to Italy, because he wants to live in America with her—and is insulted that she would suggest he just wants the necessary papers to stay in the country. They talk about Eddie, then Beatrice, and finally Rodolpho coaxes Catherine into joining him in the bedroom.

Eddie appears on the street, drunk. He goes in the house, and Catherine emerges from the bedroom straightening her dress. When Rodolpho soon also emerges, Eddie tells him to leave immediately, without Catherine. She objects, but he seizes her and kisses her on the lips; when Rodolpho tries to intervene, Eddie grabs him, holds him for a moment, and kisses him too. Believing he has proven something, he reasserts his order for Rodolpho to leave, alone, then stumbles out.

Alfieri reports that he next saw Eddie on December 27, when their exchange left Alfieri feeling strangely powerless. Eddie enters the office, and the conversation picks up with Alfieri asking about Rodolpho's refusing to leave. After Eddie sticks to his talking points about his responsibility toward Catherine and Rodolpho's insufficiently masculine nature, Alfieri begs him one last time to leave them alone; to do otherwise will only alienate him from everyone around him. Eddie leaves, stubborn, and Alfieri follows, calling to him hopelessly.

Eddie appears at the phone booth. He calls the Immigration Bureau and reports, anonymously, the pair of undocumented men staying on the ground floor of 441 Saxon Street in Brooklyn. After hanging up, he passes Louis and Mike on the street. Eddie enters his house, where Beatrice is packing up Christmas decorations. She has already helped her cousins move to Mrs. Dondero's apartment upstairs. When Eddie starts up about restraining Catherine's activities, Beatrice loses her temper. Puffing his chest, Eddie vaguely demands respect, finally saying that he is tired of the questions about what he does or does not want to do in the bedroom. Eddie tries to blame her for having changed and demands that she take him at his word no matter what. As for Catherine, Beatrice points out that if he had not sheltered her so much, she might not have fallen in love with the first decent and interesting man who happened along. He tries to suggest that he will let her go out in the evenings now, but she points out that it is too late. She tries to persuade him to go to their niece's wedding next week. When Catherine comes down, Beatrice gets her and Eddie to reconcile for the moment. Catherine gets permission to bring more pillowcases upstairs for the two other boarders also there, but Eddie suddenly objects to putting all the submarines—a term for those arriving belowdecks as undocumented immigrants—together.

Two immigration officers knock, and Eddie instructs Catherine to run up the fire escape and lead

Marco and Rodolpho out. She is confused and upset, but the officers start hollering, and she rushes out. The officers enter, sweep around the apartment, then split up to head upstairs via both the inside and outside stairways. Soon after, the officers, the four Italians, and Catherine come down the stairs, with Catherine pleading desperately for Rodolpho's freedom. When he gets a chance, Marco breaks free in order to spit in Eddie's face. Enraged, Eddie starts yelling, but when they get outside, Marco publicly accuses Eddie of killing his children (by ruining Marco's chances of continuing to send money home to them). All the neighbors, including Mr. Lipari, Louis, and Mike, walk away, ignoring Eddie's pleas for sympathy. Still enraged, Eddie says he will kill Marco.

The lights rise on a prison reception room (perhaps, depending on the performance, the same desk used to represent Alfieri's office). Alfieri insists that Marco agree not to commit any crimes before he bails him out. Rodolpho insists too, even though Marco's deportation is certain, so that Marco can work in the meantime. Rodolpho and Catherine will solve things for him by marrying.

In the apartment, Eddie is in his rocker, and Beatrice appears in fine clothes. She says she is going out, but Eddie reiterates his decision that if she goes, she can never come back. Catherine appears and says they need to get going because the priest will not wait; when Beatrice says Catherine should go without her, Catherine berates Eddie for his selfishness. Rodolpho arrives, ominously indicating that Marco is coming—as soon as he finishes praying. Catherine and Beatrice start begging Eddie to leave, and Rodolpho offers a humble apology for any wrongdoing, but Eddie remains indignant and unyielding over Marco's insults. Marco arrives outside and vindictively calls to Eddie, who steps outside. Eddie demands a public apology from Marco, then promptly attacks him, but Marco fends him off with a blow to the neck and calls Eddie an animal. Eddie takes out a knife, and Louis tries to intercede, but Eddie raises the knife threateningly. Marco still will not apologize, so Eddie rushes him, but Marco manages to deflect and redirect his arm so that Eddie stabs himself, falling to the ground. Eddie dies in Beatrice's arms.

Alfieri steps out of the crowd to deliver an epilogue about respecting Eddie, to an extent, for living out his feelings to the fullest—though "it is better to settle for half"—and about his mourning Eddie with a sense of alarm.

Characters

Mr. Alfieri

The lawyer who narrates the drama is in his fifties and somehow feels an important connection with Brooklyn's Red Hook area. His wife and friends think he should prefer something classier, but he realizes that laborers like Eddie are the sorts who do not just "settle for half" when it comes to engaging with life, and he appreciates that. Still, he laments that he felt powerless to alter the course of Eddie's life— and death—despite his repeated efforts to persuade Eddie to just let go of Catherine. Alfieri even quite forthrightly suggests that there is something unwholesome about Eddie's affection for Catherine—that he loves her more than an uncle should love a niece—but it seems Eddie is too wrapped up in that love to let the admonition sink in. For Alfieri to have pressed the point further might have risked an explosion of violence then and there, especially given how Eddie reacts "*furiously*" when Alfieri insinuates that deep down Eddie wants to marry Catherine himself. After all, Alfieri is only a lawyer, not a psychotherapist.

Tony Bereli

Tony is the friend—and apparent Mafia connection—who ushers Marco and Rodolpho to Eddie and Beatrice's doorstep and also coordinates their work situation.

Beatrice Carbone

Eddie's spouse is, as was common in that era, largely constrained to the role of housewife; that is, Eddie does his best to constrain her to that role. But she clearly has her own opinions and understands the complicated family situation far better than Eddie realizes, leading her to urge Catherine to take advantage of Rodolpho's wholehearted affections and get out of the house while she can. Beatrice is surely partly hoping that Catherine's departure will encourage Eddie to refocus his romantic energy toward his wife, as he most certainly ought to. For all his difficulties and challenges, Beatrice greatly mourns her husband's death.

Eddie Carbone

Eddie and his complicated psychology are at the center of the play. Here he is, having helped raise his niece in place of her deceased parents, and all he wants, or so he thinks, is what is best for her. As affectionate parents or surrogate parents are liable to do, however, he believes that what is best for her is sheltering her and shielding her from all the possibilities in the world. Now comes along a charming young gentleman whom she falls for, and Eddie cannot stand the idea of her running off with him—because Rodolpho's situation as an immigrant seems too desperate, and Rodolpho himself seems, in Eddie's bigoted opinion, insufficiently manly.

Eddie takes this as evidence that Rodolpho "ain't right"—that is, that he is homosexual—and cannot be serious about his affection for Catherine. Unfortunately, Eddie gets too bottled up in his own ill-informed perspective, his indignity over the situation gradually turns to rage, and when his rage gets redirected toward himself, he dies.

Catherine "Katie"

Catherine is usually called "Katie" by her aunt and uncle, Beatrice and Eddie, who have raised her since an unspecified age. Katie has reached a level of maturity that means she is ready to go out into the world and not only meet people but also explore her own identity through relationships with them. The only problem is that her uncle has grown too attached to her and does not want to let her engage in that exploration. Beatrice does not exactly blame Katie for her uncle's attachment, but she does point out that sitting on the tub to chat with Eddie while he shaves in his underwear, for example, as well as walking around the house in her slip, makes the wrong impression, or sends the wrong message, or no longer seems appropriate—or all of the above. As a young girl, of course, Katie could be close with her uncle in an entirely innocent way, and, as she aged, she maintained this innocence about the relationship. But Katie realizes that Beatrice is right about her needing to get out of the house when the drunken Eddie seizes and kisses her on the lips, in what amounts to an act of sexual assault. As Katie later implicitly but caustically informs him, with this heinous act he lost any right to reprimand anybody else about their actions, and at this point she is finally indeed more than happy to get out of the house. Nevertheless, like Beatrice, she mourns Eddie's death.

Charley

The character identified in the script as the First Immigration Officer is named Charley. The two officers are quite efficient at getting their job done, covering the escape routes in the apartment building so that the men they are seeking are effectively trapped inside.

Dominick

The Second Immigration Officer is named Dominick.

Mrs. Dondero

Not appearing in the play, Mrs. Dondero is the older woman upstairs with extra space to rent out to Marco and Rodolpho as well as the two newcomers.

Mr. and Mrs. Lipari

Mr. Lipari is the neighborhood butcher, and a nephew of his is one of the newly arrived men rounded up by the immigration officers. When Eddie pleads with him not to believe Marco's accusation, Mr. Lipari and his wife simply turn away. This does not exactly bear out Eddie's earlier heated suggestion that the Lipari family is bad-tempered.

Louis

A fellow longshoreman of Eddie's, Louis always hangs out with Mike. They like to go bowling.

Marco

An Italian mason and general handyman, Marco, alongside his younger brother, Rodolpho, goes to work as a common docks laborer upon his arrival in the United States. His wife and three children back in Sicily are essentially starving, and at least one seems to have tuberculosis, so he has come to the United States to try to earn and send home as much money as possible. Referred to only as the "syndicate" in the play, the Mafia are the ones who have arranged the brothers' illegal immigration and daily work. Marco is immensely strong but also described in the stage directions as "*tender*" and "*quietvoiced.*" He is friendly with his cousin Beatrice and her husband, but when he and Rodolpho are rounded up by immigration officers, Marco quickly realizes that Eddie—who had made clear his hostility toward Rodolpho—was responsible. It is not clear whether Marco is intent on taking his revenge to the level of murder: he ultimately engages in a fight with Eddie without bearing any weapons and turns Eddie's knife back on himself only in what seems like legitimate self-defense.

Mike

A friend of Louis and Eddie's, Mike enjoys bowling. When he recalls all the funny things Rodolpho has said and done, he can hardly stop laughing.

Nancy

Catherine's mother, Nancy, was Beatrice's sister. Eddie suggests that he is the one who specifically promised to the dying Nancy that he would be responsible for her daughter, Katie. It would seem more likely that Nancy would have expected such a promise from her sister, Beatrice—but it is possible that Nancy was enough under the sway of patriarchal American culture to consider Beatrice's husband the one in the position of ultimate authority in the relationship. Or perhaps Eddie simply assumed that authority for himself and made a promise that the dying Nancy did not need or even want from him in particular.

Rodolpho

Marco's brother, Rodolpho, is, quite simply, the most pleasant person in the play. He is always quick with smiles, laughs, buoyant comments, and a positive attitude. Liable to burst into song among the presumably stoical, practical longshoremen at the docks, he delights even them. Eddie fears that this delight is actually derogatory—that everyone is laughing *at* Rodolpho for acting so differently from them. He especially fears that this difference is a sign of homosexuality. But when Eddie speaks with Louis and Mike, itis not at all clear that Mike's delight carries any derogatory sense. In Mike's words, when Rodolpho's around, "everybody's happy." It is, in fact, comically ironic that Eddie should think that there is something wrong with someone because he makes everyone around him happy. Although Eddie refuses to believe it, by the play's end it seems clear that Rodolpho truly loves Catherine and wants to spend his life with her.

Two "Submarines"

As they are called in the dramatis personae (the list of characters at the beginning of the script), the Two "Submarines," or undocumented immigrants, who take refuge in Mrs. Dondero's apartment include a nephew of Mr. Lipari's.

Patriarchy

From early in the opening scene, it is apparent that the Carbone household is under the influence of ideas of patriarchy—that the man who earns the money considers himself the one in charge and expects his word to amount to law. Eddie's dominating words and actions make this perfectly clear, but it is also apparent in the attitudes of Catherine and Beatrice. Whether or not they believe that men should hold all positions of authority and women should defer to them, they have little choice but to function in both a society and a family organized as such. Catherine evidently possesses an extraordinary intelligence, one allowing her to graduate from high school at the age of sixteen and be on the verge of graduating at the top of her class in stenographer's school at the age of seventeen. And yet if she performs so well intellectually, the modern reader wonders, why is she only going to stenographer's school?

One reason is that in the 1950s, when the play is understood to be set, many colleges did not yet admit women, especially into programs for white-collar professions. On top of this, perhaps stenographer's school is all Eddie could afford—or all he cared to decide that he could afford. Thus, the highly intelligent Catherine is delighted at the prospect of getting a stenographer's job at a plumbing company, while Beatrice is delighted at the prospect that "some day she could be a secretary." Only in a painfully patriarchal society must intelligent women be content to aim so low in their professional lives.

Topics for Further Study

- Do some investigation into the psychological theories of Sigmund Freud, and then write a paper examining the inner workings of Eddie's mind from a Freudian perspective. If possible, find a way to explain Alfieri's notion that people usually "settle for half" in Freudian terms.

- The title of Miller's play *A View from the Bridge* bears little relation to the action, with the only prominent mention of a bridge coming in Alfieri's reference to the Brooklyn Bridge in his opening monologue. Write a paper in which you reflect on the connotations and possible meanings of the title, researching and elaborating on the symbolic, philosophical, and existential significance of bridges as appropriate.

- Read the young-adult novel *Mafia Girl* (2015), by Deborah Blumenthal, which follows the very interesting Manhattan life of Mia, who is the daughter of a notorious Mafia boss—and who develops affection for a police officer. Then write an essay in which you compare and contrast the situations of Mia and Catherine with respect to developing romantic sentiments that run counter to their fathers' (or, in Catherine's case, father figure's) interests. Conclude by offering your opinion about which young woman's situation is more difficult and why.

- Write one more scene to attach to the end of *A View from the Bridge* to depict where the surviving characters' lives will take them next. You may need to do a little research about 1950s America for clues and guidance. You can pick up right where the play leaves off, with Beatrice and Catherine embracing the dying Eddie in the street, or start with a fresh scene. Once the scene is written, recruit a few classmates to act out and film it, and share it with the class. Post the video online and allow your classmates to comment.

Father-Child Relationships

In the context of the family, there might be such a thing as a benevolent patriarchy, with a husband and father who cares about everyone and, though recognized as the family's ultimate authority, believes in equality of influence between himself and his wife. Eddie is no such husband—and ultimately no father at all to the niece he has raised like a daughter. It is bad enough that he belittles the seventeen-year-old young woman as "kid" when he is in the process of judging her for the clothes she favors. It is worse that he embarrasses her in front of company by not only insisting that she change her shoes but, indeed, effectively insisting that she do so without his needing to make the demand explicit, placing her in the position of mutely deferential servant. And it is both terrible and terrifying that he thinks—while drunk—that his position gives him any right to seize his grown niece and force a kiss from her. It seems that the sense of patriarchy is rooted so deeply in his mind that he literally believes that whatever he thinks or wants to do is "right." It goes to show how easily patriarchy can evolve into outright tyranny.

An interesting thing about drama, as well as fiction, is that the author may only be attempting to truthfully portray a single, unique situation involving a particular group of people, but presenting an audience with that portrayal can make certain generalized statements whether the author intended it or not. Specifically here, Eddie is a man who is not related to Catherine by blood—she is his wife's sister's daughter. Miller, then, might be seen as suggesting that such a situation is in part problematic because the incest taboo is a step removed—the essential blood relation is lacking. Indeed, in an interview with Ronald Hayman, Miller reported that versions of the story he heard from Longhi seemed to be well known in Italian American circles, as if it were a folktale, with "the orphan girl or the niece who is not quite a blood relation living in the house" being a fixed element. In the play, Miller hints at the seriousness of such a problem in having Eddie simply kiss Catherine, but this speaks to situations where the abuse is far more serious. The play functions as a warning, then, about situations where a controlling and possessive man ends up having an intimate relationship with a young woman who is not his own daughter. People's looking out for each other—as Beatrice looks out for Catherine—is an important means of preventing sexual abuse and assault.

Immigrant Life

In what begins in an entirely different type of story from that of Eddie and Catherine's relationship, Beatrice's cousins arrive in Brooklyn as immigrants from Italy. Miller says much about how difficult—as well as promising—life can be for such immigrants, whether they are documented or not. Marco's situation at home is as desperate as a situation can be: there is not enough work to be done back in Sicily, and so he cannot make enough money to adequately feed his family. It may be risky to slip into a country without proper documentation and try to make a living there, but with a little help getting overseas passage and work once arrived, it can be done. The upside of the risk is made clear when Marco starts to make enough money to ensure that his wife and children are getting both food and medicine. The downside includes the cramped living quarters and the humble occupations that immigrants end up in—occupations that need no training and likely pay a low wage, since employers can take advantage of the fact that undocumented immigrants have no legal recourse for demanding higher wages. Some people reflexively feel that undocumented immigrants, having broken the rules of entry, have literally no right to exist in the country where they find themselves, meaning if they are found, they should be deported. In taking a humanistic view of immigration, Miller's play makes a profound statement in favor of the acceptance of undocumented immigrants.

Justice

Although the events never reach the courtroom, Miller's play ends up hinging on concepts of justice. Alfieri makes a point, in his opening monologue, of mentioning, "Justice is very important here." He also subtly makes the more controversial point that the law alone cannot be expected to ensure justice in the world. He says, "Oh, there were many here who were justly shot by unjust men," suggesting that even though the men enacting the punishment were themselves neither official nor unofficial upholders of the law, the punishment inflicted—such as on gangsters like "Frankie Yale"—was, in itself, just. In other words, sometimes, as the lawyer Alfieri suggests, regardless of what the law says, it may be fair for people to take justice into their own hands.

This is what Marco does, or means to do, in his antagonism toward Eddie. Marco declares his conviction that among honorable men, and in particular according to Sicilian codes of family honor, Eddie would not be left alive after his betrayal of his wife's two cousins. Marco realizes that being sent back to Italy will ensure that he will once again be unable to provide for his family, quite possibly leading to their premature deaths. The presence of the other two submarines in the building makes Eddie's betrayal worse, since two additional men against whom Eddie has no right to hold a grudge will likely also not be able to provide for themselves and their families. Marco's sense of honor, his sense of justice, prods him not only to spit in Eddie's face and make a public accusation with regard to the unjust betrayal but also to summon him to a showdown. Even then, obstinately holding his ground, Eddie gives himself an unfair advantage with the knife. The audience may, indeed should, mourn Eddie's lost life, but many may feel that, for putting so many immigrants at risk for no other reason than his own petty and bigoted resentments, Eddie deserves to die. Importantly, though, this sentence was carried out not by Marco —who declined to try to commit coldblooded murder, which would have remained a morally questionable act—but, in effect, by fate.

Style

Foreshadowing

In telling the tragic story of Eddie's demise retrospectively, as a memory recalled at a later time, Alfieri gives almost nothing away—except for the fact that the end is a tragic one. At the end of his opening monologue, he vaguely reveals that there was some complaint that left him feeling powerless, unable to do anything but watch "it run its bloody course." With such an introduction to the drama, most audience members will be looking, whether intentionally or not, for the seeds of the problem and how it might lead to a violent end, which may or may not involve someone's death. This foreshadowing, ensuring that the audience's senses are primed from the beginning, allows Miller to be subtle with the action as it proceeds.

The dramatic action is fairly subdued through the early scenes—people are interacting, and they do not always agree, but it is hard to see how anyone involved could be moved to violence. An audience member might even lament that there is not enough action in these early scenes, but the prospect that some violence will indeed occur helps sustain interest. The characters gradually reveal antagonisms that are liable to deepen over time, and Alfieri also steps in several more times to help advance the narrative—and drop further foreshadowing hints about what will take place. At one point he mentions that Eddie in particular has "a destiny" to fulfill, which leaves Eddie with potentially either a subjective or an objective role to fill—he might be either the inflicter or the victim of violence (and turns out to be both). Later Alfieri narrates, after a visit from Eddie, that he "could have finished the whole story that afternoon." By now the audience or reader realizes that Eddie is going to do something of great consequence, but tension remains about what that something will be.

Stage Directions

Dramatists almost invariably use stage directions to indicate the physical actions taking place on the stage, including gestures and facial expressions. Some of Miller's directions here are intriguing because, rather than simply indicating outward action, he describes the innermost feelings and mind-sets of the characters. For example, when Eddie is finally relenting with regard to Catherine's desire to get a job, he is said to deliver one of his lines "*with a sense of her childhood, her babyhood, and the years.*" The line itself is only "All right, go to work," but the specificity of the direction speaks to the deeper emotional sense underlying the otherwise nondescript line. Similarly, when the Carbones are asking Beatrice's cousins about their home back in Italy, Rodolpho delivers a line not just while smiling, but while "*smiling at the smallness of his town.*" This detailed description might seem unnecessary, because the line that follows makes the sense fairly clear: "In our town there are no piers, only the beach, and little fishing boats." But Miller's specificity indicates that he has a most complete image of the dramatic action in his mind, and the smile he describes is indeed a very specific kind of smile—not just a proud smile, as one might otherwise imagine—and for the reader, at least, recognizing the fullness of Miller's vision can evoke confidence in his dramatic talents and in this play in particular.

Theatrical Fluidity

As is often done with a large enough stage, Miller's play calls for it to be divided up into several different scenes, so that dramatic action can take place in several different locales without any need for curtain use or prop rearrangement. As convenient as this is, it also calls for a slightly higher level of dramatic talent on the part of the actors, especially, in this case, Alfieri. On several occasions, he must turn from narrating the play while facing the audience to engaging with another character visiting his office. This must be done in a way that allows the audience to understand the distinction between the modes of his speech, perhaps with some assistance from lighting, and also retains their suspension of disbelief with regard to the "reality" of what is taking place.

To Red Hook, From Sicily

The Brooklyn neighborhood of Red Hook—located on the western coast of the borough, adjacent to Governors Island and opposite the Statue of Liberty—was a thriving seaport through the early twentieth century. The area was first named Roode Hoek by the Dutch for the hooklike shape of the peninsula protruding into Upper New York Bay and for the redness of the soil found there. Settled as a village in the seventeenth century, it became an especially important port in the mid-nineteenth century with the opening of the Atlantic Basin, an artificial harbor, in 1847. On the south side of the hook, the similar Erie Basin opened in 1864, with Red Hook becoming the end point of shipping going up and down the Erie Canal.

Meanwhile through the end of the nineteenth century, the essentially feudal society that persisted in southern Italy meant that life was extremely difficult for peasants, and by the turn of the twentieth century they were seeking passage to America in droves. The southern mountain region of Basilicata, for one, lost some 40 percent of its population to emigration between 1906 and 1915. Life was especially difficult for many in Sicily, where the influence of the Mafia had been growing since the early nineteenth century. With secretive, communitybased hierarchies of individuals gaining widespread control of businesses and governmental positions—such as by hiring or appointing only people associated with their organization— profits from the daily economy as well as influxes of governmental investment in infrastructure were siphoned through Mafia members' selfserving hands, leaving that much less for the common people. Mafia job preferment and the slow ruination of the economy meant that work grew scarce for those without connections, leaving the unemployment rate consistently hovering around 30 percent, a devastating proportion.

Compare & Contrast

- **1950s:** With over twenty thousand residents, many of whom work the docks and about half whom live in public housing, Red Hook is cut off from the rest of Brooklyn by a highway and is known as a tough area—sometimes called a slum— where Italian American gangsters thrive.

  Today: Having seen its docks eclipsed by larger-scale waterfront operations elsewhere, Red Hook, now home to just over ten thousand residents, has recently seen a modest resurgence with the relocation of middleclass artists, technology firms, and creative companies to the area. One of the key harbors was bought out and taken over by an Ikea furniture superstore.

- **1950s:** As of 1950, more than 1.4 million individuals who were born in Italy are residing in the United States. The figure has been slowly dropping since the mid-1930s, when more restrictive immigration policies were put in place. Special allowance is made for immigration from Italy, which is still suffering from defeat in World War II, from 1952 to 1962, and through those decades, there are more foreign-born Americans from Italy than from any other nation.

  Today: Although immigration policies opened back up in 1965, the years of peak migration from Italy had already passed. The number of foreign-born Italian Americans reached a low of 580,000 in 1990, climbing back up to just over 600,000 in 2000. As of the year 2000, New York State is home to over 2.7 million Italian Americans.

- **1950s:** In an era inhibited by suburban religious values as well as Cold War fears, many homosexual people remain closeted. But milestones in the 1950s, including the publication of a book about homosexuals as a national minority, the formation of gay support organizations, and the extensive sexuality research conducted by Dr. Alfred Kinsey and his associates, pave the way for wider understanding and appreciation of homosexuality and sexual difference.

Today: Laws forbidding homosexual activity have been struck down across America, the Supreme Court legalized gay marriage nationwide in 2015, pride parades are common in urban centers and elsewhere, many high-profile celebrities have publicly revealed their sexual preferences, and with the additional support of social media, more people than ever are empowered to be forthright about and happy with their sexual orientation no matter what it is.

The occasional involvement of Mafia-linked figures in crimes in America, including violent crimes, contributed to stereotypes regarding the character of Italians generally. American officials eager to find a basis for discrimination were able to rely on the theories of the racist northern Italian doctor Cesare Lombroso, who concluded through measurements of body parts, including heads (a practice called phrenology, which has long since been dismissed as a pseudoscience), that southern Italians were inherently inclined toward criminality. Thus did the US Immigration Commission's 1911 Dillingham report, cited by Helene Stapinski in the *New York Times*, conclude, "Certain kinds of criminality are inherent in the Italian race. In the popular mind, crimes of personal violence, robbery, blackmail and extortion are peculiar to the people of Italy." The commission had been further encouraged to stem Italian immigration by Italian politicians who realized that their nation was bleeding manpower at an incredible rate, thanks to conditions that left the common people "suffering" and "starving," in Stapinski's words.

All this ultimately led to the Immigration Act of 1924—referred to by Eddie in Miller's play as "the Immigration Law"—which cut immigration from Italy by some 90 percent. Naturally, this meant that emigration from Italy, which remained necessary for many under the intolerable conditions there, was put more in the control of organized crime, increasing the Mafia's influence in America. Not until after World War II, when Italian Americans served in the military in disproportionately high numbers, did the Italian character—outside of organized crime, that is—gain favor and respect in the popular American imagination.

For all its success as a port, Red Hook became

dominated by the sorts of Italian Americans who found themselves atop the hierarchy of organized crime and thus gained a reputation as an especially tough part of the city. As Alfieri reports in the beginning of *A View from the Bridge*, Al Capone and Frankie Yale were just two of the best-known mobsters who graced (so to speak) the streets of the district. In light of the abundance of low-income dockworkers and their families, the area became home to one of the first federal housing projects in 1938, the Red Hook Houses. By 1950, some twenty-one thousand residents were compressed into Red Hook; for comparison's sake, the population was down to eleven thousand in the early twenty-first century. Also by 1950, however, the area was becoming increasingly isolated, by virtue of the construction of the Gowanus Expressway in 1946 and the Brooklyn Battery Tunnel in 1950, both of which cut Red Hook off from mainland Brooklyn. Moreover, shipping practices shifted to the use of large metal containers that required more dock space and fewer dockhands, and ports developing in New Jersey began to thrive. The culture of Italian American longshoremen in Red Hook had seen its peak.

Critical Overview

Although Miller Is Now Regarded As One Of The Greatest Playwrights In American History, Critics In His Era Were Not Always Favorable Toward Him, Whether Due To His Politics, His Personal Life, Their Own Expectations, Or, On Occasion, The Actual Quality Of The Play In Question. Coming A Half Decade After Miller'S 1949 Masterpiece *Death Of A Salesman, A View From The Bridge* found a critical community primed to judge his work with the highest of standards. In the *New York Daily News*, John Chapman called the play a "modern classic," observing, "What happens in it simply has to happen, and this is the inevitability of true tragedy." Chapman declared:

> This is an intensely absorbing drama, sure of itself every step of the way. It makes no false moves, wastes no time and has the beauty that comes from directness and simplicity…. Miller has come a long way in our theatre, and he will go much farther, for his mind is a mind that won't stay still.

Walcot Gibbs, in the *New Yorker*, was generally appreciative, admiring the "broken rhythms and mindless repetitions" that lend a "grotesque eloquence" to the characters' working-class speech. The reviewer adds that Miller's "command of the idiom is nearly perfect and his treatment of the dramatic incident is beyond criticism." Leonard Moss, writing in 1980 in *Arthur Miller*, would show similar admiration for the subtlety of the dialogue in *A View from the Bridge*. He observes that the scene introducing Marco and Rodolpho "splendidly illustrates Miller's ability to encompass strong anxiety in commonplace talk." In the same vein, once the false love triangle develops, "the inception of the sex-rivalry is conveyed entirely through Eddie's ominous silences and through the connotations of his sullen dialogue."

Gibbs's one major complaint, echoed by Moss, was that Alfieri makes for an unnecessary and somewhat unwelcome narrator, as if Miller felt a need to dress up his humble play in fancier clothes to make it more acceptable to elitist audiences. Gibbs notes of Alfieri, "It was my feeling that he served merely to bring a superfluous and rather pretentious air of classroom erudition to an otherwise admirably forthright play." He affirmed that the excellent play needed no such "genteel embroidery." Moss suggests that, even though Alfieri effectively serves the classical function of the Greek chorus, he is found "constantly interrupting the cumulation of tension," and overall his "contribution … seems seriously limited."

The expanded two-act version of *A View from the Bridge* debuted in London in 1956, and Samantha Ellis, in a 2003 retrospective for the London *Guardian*—after pointing out that Marilyn Monroe stole the show on opening night in a scarlet satin gown—quotes several reviewers' opinions of the production. As quoted by Ellis, Milton Shulman of the *Evening Standard* found the play "so bulging with dramatic muscles that it is constantly on the verge of bursting its seams." *Sunday Times* reviewer Harold Hobson, Ellis writes, who had seen the New York production and considered it a "masterpiece," was slightly less pleased with the London version, writing: "It has been decorated. Things which brooded in the dark recesses of undefined feeling have been brought into the light." The playwright's communication with the audience, he felt, amounted to "special pleading; though the special pleading is very good."

Like Gibbs, a London *Times* reviewer (also quoted by Ellis) found that Alfieri's narration contributed to the result's being "a good picture in a pretentious frame." In the reviewer's opinion, the play represented "the miscarriage of an intention to elevate these ordinary men and women to the rank of heroes and heroines of high tragedy." Far more positively, Ellis reports that Kenneth Tynan, writing in the *Observer*, found the London production "uncannily good" and the play itself "just short of being a masterpiece." Ellis also notes that Cecil Wilson, writing in the *Daily Mail*, considered the play "savage, searing and spellbinding," a work that "though no shocker, will shake you to the core." James J. Martine, in an introduction to the 1979 collection *Critical Essays on Arthur Miller*, sums up the playwright's importance in stating, "Miller is one of the most important dramatists of this century."

What Do I Read Next?

- Like this play, Miller's Pulitzer-and Tonywinning masterpiece, *Death of a Salesman* (1949), also deals with the end of an era for a certain breed of conventional, patriarchal husband and father. The play's runaway success immortalized the tragic character of Willy Loman, a salesman in his early sixties who finds himself flummoxed by reality.

- The seedier side of Brooklyn was immortalized in Hubert Selby Jr.'s perceptive novel *Last Exit to Brooklyn* (1964), which zeroes in on Red Hook dockworkers, union corruption, and underworld violence.

- American novelist William Styron

made his debut with *Lie Down in Darkness* (1951), a book revolving around a relationship between a father and a daughter in which the former harbors too much love for the latter, with ultimately tragic consequences.

- Miller and director Elia Kazan were once friends and associates—until Kazan chose to name names when he was brought before the House Un-American Activities Committee in 1952, four years before Miller. The two had been collaborating on a screenplay for an anti-union-corruption film set in Red Hook, called "The Hook," but it never got made. Kazan, however, went on to direct the similarly set but anti-Communist film *On the Waterfront* (1954), which brought Marlon Brando to fame. The screenplay was written by Budd Schulberg, who went on to publish both *On the Waterfront: A Screenplay* (1981) and *On the Waterfront: A Play* (2001), the latter coauthored with Stan Silverman.

- Miller has said that one drama in particular made an especially profound impression on him during his university days: Norwegian playwright Henrik Ibsen's *A Doll's House* (1879). The play is distinctly feminist in an era before feminism was even a word, promoting freedom of action for a married woman in oppressive patriarchal circumstances.

- An American teenager who gets involved with an Italian who may or may not be trouble is also a feature of Kristin Rae's young-adult romance *Wish You Were Italian* (2014), in which Pippa's parents send her to Florence, Italy, to attend art school, but Pippa is more interested in having nonacademic cross-cultural experiences.

- *Images of Red Hook, Brooklyn* (2012), by Thomas Rupolo, provides some 120 photographs of the neighborhood, ranging from the distant past to the present, along with a brief history, informative captions, and commentary from residents and laborers who have known the area best.

- Enoch Brater's *Arthur Miller: A Playwright's Life and Works* (2005) is among the most recent treatments of the important events in Miller's life as well as the cultural relevance of his writings.

Sources

"Arthur Miller, Legendary American Playwright, Is Dead," In *New York Times*, February 11, 2005, http://www.nytimes.com/2005/02/11/theater/arthur-miller-legendary-american-playwright-is-dead.html (accessed July 1, 2017).

Carson, Neil, *Arthur Miller*, Grove Press, 1982, pp. 1–13.

Cavaioli, Frank J., "Patterns of Italian Immigration to the United States," in *Catholic Social Science Review*, Vol. 13, 2008, pp. 213–29, https://www.pdcnet.org/collection/fshow?id=cssr_2008_0013_0213_0229&file_type=pdf (accessed July 4, 2017).

Chapman, John, Review of *A View from the Bridge*, in *File on Miller*, compiled by C. W. E. Bigsby, Methuen, 1988, p. 37; originally published in *New York Daily News*, September 30, 1955.

Ellis, Samantha, "*A View from the Bridge*, October 1956," in *Guardian* (London, England), July 16, 2003, https://www.theguardian.com/stage/2003/jul/16/thea (accessed July 1, 2017).

Gibbs, Walcot, Review of *A View from the Bridge*, in *File on Miller*, compiled by C. W. E. Bigsby, Methuen, 1988, pp. 37–38; originally published in *New Yorker*, October 8, 1955.

Hayman, Ronald, "Interview," in *Conversations*

with Arthur Miller, edited by Matthew C. Roudané, University Press of Mississippi, 1987, p. 192; originally published in *Arthur Miller*, Heinemann, 1970.

"LGBT History Month: The 1950s and the Roots of LGBT Politics," Human Rights Campaign website, October 10, 2014, http://www.hrc.org/blog/lgbt-historymonth-the-1950s-and-the-roots-of-lgbt-politics (accessed July 3, 2017).

"The Mafia," Best of Sicily, http://www.bestofsicily.com/mafia.htm (accessed July 2, 2017).

Martine, James J., *Critical Essays on Arthur Miller*, G. K. Hall, 1979, p. xxii.

"Masculinity, Gender Roles, and T.V. Shows from the 1950s," in *Artifice*, October 18, 2014, https://the-artifice.com/masculinity-gender-roles-tv-1950s/ (accessed July 3, 2017).

Miller, Arthur, *A View from the Bridge*, in *Arthur Miller: Eight Plays*, Nelson Doubleday, 1981, pp. 393–470.

Morris, Bonnie J., "History of Lesbian, Gay & Bisexual Social Movements,"http://www.apa.org/pi/lgbt/resources/hi (accessed July 3, 2017).

Moss, Leonard, *Arthur Miller*, rev. ed., Twayne Publishers, 1980, pp. 1–10, 44–49.

"The 1950s–1960s," in *Italian Tribune*, August 24, 2016, http://www.italiantribune.com/the-1950s-1960s/ (accessed July 2, 2017).

"Red Hook," South Brooklyn Network, http://www.southbrooklyn.com/neighborhood/redho⟨ (accessed July 2, 2017).

"Red Hook History," Waterfront Barge Museum website, http://waterfrontmuseum.org/redhook-history (accessed July 2, 2017).

"Red Hook Justice," PBS website, http://www.pbs.org/independentlens/redhookjustice/ (accessed July 2, 2017).

Stapinski, Helene, "When America Barred Italians," in *New York Times*, June 2, 2017, https://www.nytimes.com/2017/06/02/opinion/illega immigration-italianamericans.html (accessed July 2, 2017).

"*A View from the Bridge*," in *File on Miller*, compiled by C. W. E. Bigsby, Methuen, 1988, pp. 36–39.

Wertheim, Albert, "*A View from the Bridge*," in *The Cambridge Companion to Arthur Miller*, 2nd ed., edited by Christopher Bigsby, Cambridge University Press, 2010, pp. 104–17.

Further Reading

Gilbert, James, *Men In The Middle: Searching For Masculinity In The 1950S*, University of Chicago Press, 2005.

> Gilbert delves into the roles that mass media played in both promoting male conformity and introducing people to differences in ways that laid the groundwork for the social revolution of the 1960s. Among the celebrated men focused on are playwright Tennessee Williams and sex researcher Alfred Kinsey.

Mello, William J., *New York Longshoremen: Class and Power on the Docks*, University Press of Florida, 2010.

> Interactions between waterfront companies, union leaders, and governmental officials— especially as influenced by organized crime— made for big news at times in the twentieth century. Mello's history explores the public and private currents that determined the course of labor-related events in the city.

Miller, Arthur, *Timebends: A Life*, Grove Press, 1987.

The most definitive—and acclaimed —treatment of Miller's life is his own, written toward the end of his active writing career and reflecting not only on the events that mattered most to him but also on the broader trajectory of the American twentieth century.

Morreale, Ben, and Robert Carola, *Italian Americans: The Immigrant Experience*, Beaux Arts Editions, 2013.

In a history book full of black-and-white photographs that bring it to life, Morreale and Carola describe the course of Italians' history as a minority population contributing to the honor, success, and fascination of America.

Suggested Search Terms

Arthur Miller And A View From The Bridge A View from the Bridge AND New York OR London Red Hook AND Brooklyn

Red Hook AND waterfront

New York longshoremen

Italian American AND culture OR history Sicilian Mafia AND Brooklyn Arthur Miller AND Communism OR HUAC

Arthur Miller AND Marilyn Monroe